CEMENT MIXERS

First edition.

Dan Osier

PowerKiDS press.

New York

Published in 2014 by The Rosen Publishing Group, Inc.
29 East 21st Street, New York, NY 10010

First Edition

Editor: Amelie von Zumbusch
Book Design: Andrew Povolny

Photo Credits: Cover Zolwiks/Shutterstock.com; p. 5 Bram von Broekhoven/Shutterstock.com; p. 7 Baloncici/Shutterstock.com; p. 9 Alistair Berg/Lifesize/Getty Images; p. 11 Hybrid Images/Cultura/Getty Images; p. 13 Dorling Kindersley/Getty Images; p. 15 Robert Pernell/Shutterstock; p. 17 upthebanner/Shutterstock.com; p. 19 imageegami/Shutterstock.com; p. 21 Andy Sotiriou/The Image Bank/Getty Images; p. 23 George Marks/Hulton Archives/Getty Images.

Library of Congress Cataloging-in-Publication Data

Osier, Dan.
  Cement mixers / by Dan Osier. — First edition.
     pages cm. — (Construction site)
Includes index.
  ISBN 978-1-4777-2861-1 (library binding) — ISBN 978-1-4777-2954-0 (paperback) —
ISBN 978-1-4777-3031-7 (6-pack)
1. Concrete mixers—Juvenile literature. I. Title.
TA439.O85 2014
629.225—dc23

                                    2013019331

Manufactured in the United States of America

CPSIA Compliance Information: Batch # W14PK3: For Further Information contact Rosen Publishing, New York, New York at 1-800-237-9932

Contents

This truck is a cement mixer.

Cement mixers carry and mix **concrete**.

Concrete is a mix of cement, water, sand, and small rocks.

Cement is a powder.
Portland cement is the most
common kind.

11

The truck's **drum** holds the concrete.

The drum spins around. This keeps the concrete from getting too hard.

15

Drums spin one way to mix concrete. They spin the other way to pour it.

The concrete is poured out through **chutes**.

It gets hard slowly. It is fully hard after seven days.

Cement-mixer trucks were first made in Columbus, Ohio.

BETTER SERVICE

COLONIAL
SAND & STONE CO., Inc.

CONCRETE
MIXED IN TRANSIT

CIRCLE 5-5400

331

SERVICE

COLONIAL

23

WORDS TO KNOW

chute

concrete

drum

WEBSITES

Due to the changing nature of Internet links, PowerKids Press has developed an online list of websites related to the subject of this book. This site is updated regularly. Please use this link to access the list:
www.powerkidslinks.com/cs/cement/

INDEX